MEDICAL EXPENSE INSURANCE

STUDY MANUAL

The Health Insurance Association of America
Washington, D.C. 20004-1109
© 1997 by the Health Insurance Association of America
All rights reserved. Published 1997
Printed in the United States of America

ISBN 1-879143-41-0

TABLE OF CONTENTS

TO THE STUDENT

Our textbook *Medical Expense Insurance* will provide you with knowledge of the basic concepts of group major medical insurance and individual hospital-surgical insurance and their administration.

The **Medical Expense Insurance** textbook has been written by industry contributors who are each specialists in their field. This study manual has been developed by HIAA Insurance Education staff—persons skilled and experienced in the field of adult and industry education.

We hope that your participation in the HIAA Education Program will contribute to the broadening of your capabilities and the advancement of your career.

HOW TO USE THIS STUDY MANUAL

There are two types of knowledge you need to successfully pass this course: knowledge of the subject and knowledge of testing techniques. This study manual is designed to help you succeed in both.

However, please keep in mind that the Study Manual is not a substitute for the textbook. Remember that you are supplying the answers yourself—and that you could be wrong or be interpreting the question a different way from someone else! It would be best to compare answers with another student if possible. The Study Manual is a summary of the textbook and asks the types of questions likely to appear on the examination. But the exam may want more detail, or possibly ask something that was not covered in the Study Manual. Nothing can replace a detailed knowledge of the textbook itself.

SUGGESTIONS FOR STUDY— KNOWLEDGE OF THE SUBJECT

Examine the textbook and study manual thoroughly and set up a schedule for completing all material at least a week before the scheduled examination. You may need to divide longer chapters into smaller study units.

Time:

We suggest you set aside one week per chapter. The time you need for each chapter will vary depending on your previous knowledge of the subject. However, we cannot caution you enough on one point: HIAA textbooks try to give a picture of *industry* practice as a whole—your own company may do things differently from the description in the textbook.

Steps in Studying:

1) Read the Key Terms. Which ones don't you know? Are you clear on the differences between similar terms?

2) Read the chapter completely but quickly.

3) Re-read the Key Terms. Are there still any you are not sure of? If so, look them up in the chapter or the glossary. Can you define the differences between similar terms? If not, look them up in the chapter or glossary.

4) Answer the questions in this Study Manual without using the textbook.

5) Re-read the chapter again, more thoroughly, checking your answers in the Study Manual as you go. Fill in answers to questions you could not answer before and change answers to questions you got wrong before. (Questions in the Study Manual are in approximately the same order as the subjects appear in the textbook.) It would be helpful if you used a different color pen to correct the Study Manual (red instead of black, for instance). Then, when you use the Study Manual to study for the examination, you will know exactly where your weaknesses are and what to spend your time studying.

6) As you re-read the chapter thoroughly and check your Study Manual answers, make a note of terms or concepts that are still not clear, even after checking the textbook. Are there any parts of the textbook you think are ambiguous? Compare notes with others in your company taking the same course, your education representative, or someone who is an expert in that area in your company.

7) As you re-read the chapter thoroughly, can you find material in the textbook that has not been covered in the Study Manual? Make a note of it.

8) A week before the examination, re-read the Study Manual. Check your knowledge of the Key Terms. Look at the notes you made of material that was not covered by the Study Manual. Ask yourself what questions you might expect to find on the examination.

Stick to your schedule of one chapter a week. Do not leave reading or studying until the last minute.

What Should You Study?

The number of questions on the examination are distributed using two criteria: the length of the treatment in the text and the importance of the subject. It may take five pages to describe a complicated concept, but only one page to describe an equally important, but not as complicated, subject. If we distributed questions on the basis of length alone, the concept that took five pages would have five times as many questions. If we distributed questions on the basis of importance alone, each subject would have an equal number of questions. We distribute questions based on both criteria: length and importance. So the concept that took five pages to explain might have slightly more questions than the equally important subject that took one page to explain. The thing to remember is that just because one subject took five times as many pages to explain, there will not necessarily be five times the number of questions on that subject. Here is some more specific advice on what to study:

1) **terms**—go through the glossary carefully. Make sure you can tell the difference between closely related terms.

2) **court decisions**—our textbooks are not law books, so there are not too many. But you should know what the issue was, the decision, why this was important, what effect it had on the industry, and approximately when it took place.

3) **NAIC model laws and regulations**—The actual laws and regulations that appear as appendices are helpful, but we test on the text, not the appendices (although if something is not clear in the text, certainly use the appendices to clarify it—we do!)

4) **laws, especially federal laws**—DEFRA, COBRA, ERISA, OBRA-90, the HMO Act of 1973, etc.

5) **numbers**—Numbers appear in both the text and the charts. We do not expect you to memorize exact numbers, and there is no point in doing so since they change constantly. But we do expect you to have some idea of the magnitude—especially for comparison purposes—of certain key numbers. How many people are covered by individual health insurance? What percent of the population is that? Is this percent growing, shrinking, or stable? If the number is changing, how fast? This issue is covered in more detail in the following section, "Study Hints for HIAA Examinations."

6) **dates**—Dates and periods of time are important, especially when the payment of a claim hinges on a series of critical dates. However, as with numbers, you need dates as reference points for comparison. Dates also tell you the sequence of events, which is important for cause and effect. For some of the numbers in the text and charts, the date is important—how current is the data? Is it likely to be much different today? How fast are changes taking place?

7) **important topics that appear over and over again in different contexts**—HMOs, Medicare, federal and state regulations, different points of view (consumer, provider, payer).

8) **anything in the text with bullet points, multiple parts, multiple reasons**—This is a multiple choice test after all!

STUDY HINTS FOR HIAA EXAMINATIONS

This section explains HIAA testing procedures, dispels some of the misconceptions that may have developed concerning our exams, answers common questions, and gives a systematic explanation of the types of questions on the exams.

Can I rely on my experience alone to pass the exam?

Not necessarily. The HIAA textbooks reflect industry practices as a whole. Your experience might be with a company that departs from industry experience in one or more areas—and you might not even be aware of it. Another problem might be that your knowledge of a particular area is much deeper than the coverage given to that area in our textbook. This problem is covered in some detail in another part of this section, "Why do you have such tricky questions?"

Can I get answer keys to past exams, or to an exam I just took?

No. We have two main reasons: first, our courses qualify for continuing education credits in all but one of the states that offer such credits. Each state insurance department sets its own rules for granting credit. Many states have a requirement that answers are not to be given out to students—ever. So giving out answer keys would jeopardize our accreditation.

Secondly, our education committee and exam sub-committee have always advised against distributing answer keys. They believe that some students would be tempted to study only the old exams and ignore the textbooks as a short cut. (See section on "Should we use past exams as study aids?")

However, if there is a particular question, which, after deep reflection and thorough consultation with others, including your company Education Correspondent, still is completely baffling, you may call us and we will direct you to the page reference for an exam question. With thousands of students involved in each exam, this should obviously be a rare exception.

After my exam I checked my answers in the textbook, and I think one question had two answers that were correct (or no correct answers!). What do I do?

Again, the first step is to talk to others in your company who took that exam, or to your Education Correspondent. If you *still* think the exam is mistaken (no answer is correct, or two or more answers are correct), then you can formally challenge the question. Your challenge must be in writing, submitted through your Education Correspondent, and must reach HIAA by 4:30 PM Eastern time the next business day following the exam in question.

Make sure you give the name of the exam, the question number, and the reason you think the question is wrong (as well as your own name and your company, and the company address). All written challenges receive a written reply.

Occasionally we do eliminate certain questions from the scoring. But the time limit is important, since the exam grading and reporting process is both long and complicated. We cannot delay processing longer than necessary.

Please do not send in a challenge that simply proves that one of the choices is, in fact, a correct answer! Every question has a correct answer, and we already know which one it is!

Why are there so many questions about history?

This becomes almost a philosophical question, since in a sense everything is "history": Medicare, TEFRA, all regulations, etc. However, in a narrow sense there are some "history" questions, but statistically there are very few. Also please notice that some of the "history" questions are only superficially about a historical topic and are really asking something else altogether.

Is there a hidden pattern to the answers?

Definitely not! Our computer randomly arranges the answers within each question and thus also randomly decides the order of answers in the exam. The computer does this each time we make up an exam. For example, a certain question might have its answers arranged one way in spring 1991, and when the question appeared again in spring 1994, its answers would be in a different order. We do have an exception to this: answers that are numbers (dollars, numbers of days, etc.) or dates are always arranged in order from small/early to large/late ($50, $75, $100, $500 or May 1, May 9, May 31, June 1). By putting these answers in order, we alter the random order generated by the computer—we may, for example, change a correct answer in a question about dates from A to C. These changes usually cancel each other out—if we change one answer from A to C, another will be changed from C to A, etc. We do, however, keep an eye on the spread of A's, B's, C's, and D's: theoretically the computer could randomly generate a test that had all A's. That would be distracting to even the best students, and of course we would not allow that to happen. In fact, we do have guidelines for how many A's, B's, C's, and D's are allowed, but it is extremely rare for the computer to generate a spread of answers outside these guidelines.

Why do you ask questions about "how many" of something there is when the number in the textbook is probably out of date? Should we be expected to memorize exact numbers?

Any question that deals with "how many" is simply looking for an order of magnitude—a general idea of how many of something there is. Certainly you should have some idea of how many people are uninsured, how many health insurance companies there are, how many people have a certain kind of health insurance, and other useful numbers.

When we ask this type of question the "wrong" answers are very far from the "right" answer. We don't expect you to know exactly (no one does!) how many people are covered by managed care. But we do expect you to be able to make an estimate within 10 million or so. The wide margin also accounts for any recent changes.

For example, if we asked "How many members does the HIAA have?" we would never offer a set of answers like this:

A. 243.	But we might offer these:	A. 23.
B. 256.		B. 256
C. 265.		C. 1,817
D. 274.		D. 245,768.

Why do you have such tricky questions?

None of our questions is intended to be "tricky." Each question is very straightforward, and it is a mistake to second- or third-guess it. But there are several considerations you should be aware of. This is a long answer, but an important one!

First, each question should be taken on its own terms, and at the level of sophistication with which it was treated in the textbook. Take a question about Medicare, for example. Our textbooks discuss Medicare, usually in connection with some other concept (like coordination of benefits, or its effect on long-term care insurance). But our textbooks do not pretend to be manuals detailing every nuance of Medicare regulations. Someone taking one of our exams who has worked with Medicare for many years should have a knowledge of Medicare that goes far beyond our textbooks and exam questions. Therefore an exam question which has simply "Part B of Medicare covers purchase or rental of certain medical equipment," as an answer to a question may be not quite true to an expert in the subject—the expert may begin to think of all sorts of exceptions and qualifications. That is the wrong approach—do not take a question on your terms, but on its own terms, and those of the textbook.

Let's use a non-insurance example of "relative truth":

Where is the National Geographic Society located?

A. Washington DC.
B. Berlin.
C. Katmandu.
D. Steve's backyard.

Assuming you are taking a US test on geography, the context should give you the answer: Washington DC. But what if you were taking the same test and were German, and in fact there was a German counterpart organization in Berlin whose name in translation was "National Geographic Society," or what if you had lived in Katmandu and realized that the National Geographic Society had a research office there? Or what if you knew Steve, and realized that yes, behind his house in Gaithersburg Maryland were the main administrative offices of the National Geographic Society? None of these things should matter in the context of the question: the German, the Nepalese, and Steve's friend should all realize that this question is being asked of thousands of other people who do not share their specialized knowledge and yet are expected to select a "correct" answer. Their specialized knowledge, while useful in other contexts, is irrelevant here. And, of course there is a perfectly acceptable alternative: Washington DC.

Or, to take another question:

Where is the Pentagon located?

A. South Arlington.
B. Washington DC.
C. Langley.
D. Prince George's County.

Any resident of Washington would have no trouble in selecting A as the correct answer. Someone who had never visited Washington would be stumped. But what if we altered the question:

Where is the Pentagon located?

A. Washington DC.
B. Baltimore.
C. Richmond.
D. Annapolis.

Clearly a "wrong" answer is now "right!" It's all relative! If you return from Europe and immigration in New York asks you where you live, and you answer "Chicago," even though you live in the suburb of Oak Park, clearly you are not lying to the official—you are just gearing your answer to his frame of reference. And that is what we expect you to do on HIAA exams.

A similar situation arises in questions where the "right" answer is demonstrably "wrong." In a previous example, it was implied that HIAA has 256 members. Possibly no one really knows, on a given day, exactly how many members there are. Members join and leave on a regular basis. What are the rules for judging membership: announcement of joining or leaving? Paying dues? When does membership expire—midnight of a certain day, or noon? The closer you are to any situation, the more complicated it is. But luckily none of this matters! The exact number doesn't matter—the order of magnitude does. If, on test day, the HIAA actually had, according to the best available records, 261 members instead of 256, 256 would still be the best answer if the other choices were 23, 1817, and 245,768.

The second part to the question of "trickiness" has to do with the construction of multiple choice questions. As in the examples above, any question can be made easy or hard depending on the level of the answer expected. Even "What is your name?" might have a vast range of possible right answers, depending on the circumstances and who is asking the question. When we look for distracters, or "wrong" answers, we can use several possibilities:

1) the "right" answer, but with some essential change. The key word here is "essential;" something that makes this choice wrong in its very essence, not just in matter of degree.

2) a "wrong" answer that was discussed in the text. One past question dealt with "advantages to employers;" the text also listed "advantages to employees." By offering a "wrong" choice that was an advantage to an employee, and not to an employer, we suspected (correctly) that some students would not know the difference.

3) a "wrong" answer that "sounds" good, and even exists, but is wrong in this context. "DEFRA" should ring a bell with almost all students—the question is, which bell? "Canadian companies must submit their financial records to regulatory authorities on the feast of St. Jean Baptiste" is pure fancy. Yet it has a Canadian ring to it; after all, isn't the feast of St. Jean a holiday in Quebec? It's even in June!

4) a total nonsense answer. Again, it sounds good, but there is no such thing. For example "Schedule ZOO-3045 is used to report investment income on the annual statement of health insurance companies."

Are there any hints in the way a question is worded?

Be careful of wording and read carefully! Questions that begin with a general statement like "Premiums are. . ." or "An experience refund is. . ." mean all premiums and all experience refunds—in general. A general statement is true about all members of that class: for example, these statements about cats:

"A cat is an animal." "Cats are animals."

Not some cats, or only at certain times: these are general statements, which are always true. Other times questions will explicitly say "always" and "never."

Other questions hedge by saying "Many companies. . . ." or "In some cases. . ." This is used quite often in the textbooks, since they are trying to describe general industry practice, not necessarily what every company does. Usually the text will say something like "Many companies do X, Y, and Z." The exam question might ask,

Many companies do

    A. X.
    B. K.
    C. Q.
    D. R.

K, Q, and R were never mentioned in the text; maybe some companies do them. But clearly the answer is X.

Be careful of words like "help." There is a world of difference between "This piece completes the puzzle," and "This piece helps to complete the puzzle." In the first case, the puzzle is definitely complete; in the second, it may or may not be complete—we don't know.

"Can," "may" and other such words are also something to look for. "Cats may weigh over 20 pounds" does not mean that all cats weigh over 20 pounds, or even that any cat in existence at this moment weighs over 20 pounds.

Be careful of substituting an option for an obligation:

"A person caught littering will be fined $50 or sentenced to one day in jail." A question about this statement might be:

   What is the penalty for littering?

      A. a fine of $50 or one day in jail.
      B. a fine of $50.
      C. one day in jail.
      D. a fine of $50 and one day in jail.

Only answer A is possible. Answer B or C would mean that either the fine or the jail term would always be the punishment, and the other option would not be a possibility, when in fact it would. Answer D is also not possible; both cannot be true at the same time.

On the other hand, you should never use grammatical hints to guess at the right answer. We try to make sure questions are phrased in such a way as to eliminate this possibility, by using "a(n)" if some answers begin with a vowel and some with a consonant sound, and by using both forms of the verb if an answer could be singular or plural. This is often the case in the multiple option questions, which have a specific grammatical disclaimer in the instructions. If a question is phrased in the singular, it does not necessarily mean only one answer is possible, and vice versa.

Why do you force us to memorize the textbook? (50% of students) vs. Why isn't the answer in the textbook—are we supposed to make assumptions, inferences, and generalizations? (the other 50% of students!)

In general, questions tend to stick to the language in the textbook. This is not an effort to make students memorize the book, but simply because the textbook usually says it the best way. But many questions paraphrase the textbook, and some *do* ask for assumptions, inferences, generalizations, and judgments. The answers are still "in the book" in the sense that a reasonable person could be expected to consistently come up with the "correct" answer.

We are caught between two conflicting points of view, as are all test-makers. A test must measure what it's supposed to measure to be valid. HIAA tests knowledge of life and health insurance, and more specifically, our textbooks. We do our best to make sure the textbooks reflect the latest developments in the industry.

Beyond that, every test must also measure many skills. For example, our tests are in English. So they also measure reading speed, reading comprehension, and vocabulary. This could be a problem for some people—and not just those whose native language is not English! Math questions also involve a knowledge of arithmetic. Even filling in the circles on the answer sheet is a skill, and thus is being tested.

Should we use past exams as study aids?

Yes and no. Certainly past exams are good samples of the types of questions you can expect. However you will be sadly disappointed if you expect to see the identical questions on a future exam!! Approximately half the questions on any given exam are changed before they are used again. These modified questions then go back into our database of questions. Some of the changes may be slight—so slight you don't notice them—but most of the time they affect the answer significantly. Negative questions can turn into positive questions, and vice versa. The insertion of a word like "not" or "all" can make a correct answer wrong or a wrong answer right. What was once the correct answer can change completely (more than one right answer is usually possible, after all) and the wrong choices which seemed so silly and obvious on a past exam can be modified so that only the very best students will be able to identify them as "wrong."

Generally 20-25% of the questions on any given exam are completely new. Another 50% or so are modified questions—they have appeared in some form in past exams (during the last 15 years!) but have now been changed. That leaves 25-30% of the questions that, in fact, have appeared in identical form on past exams. But which past exam? A question could have appeared in spring 1984. . . .or fall 1989. . .or. . . . Furthermore, have you ever wondered why identical questions continue to appear? There is only one answer: they are effective questions! And effective questions separate knowledgeable students from ones who do not know the subject thoroughly.

It is a questionable use of time to go through 15 years' worth of 100-question exams in hopes of memorizing the 25-30% of repeat questions—without even knowing which ones they are and without answer keys! It would be far better to read the textbook thoroughly.

I don't have access to old exams!! What are the questions like?

Each Study Manual has sample questions, with answers, at the back.

Chapter 1

GROUP MAJOR MEDICAL EXPENSE INSURANCE

■ Key Terms

All cause

Benefit Maximum

Coinsurance

Coinsurance maximum

Common accident provision

Comprehensive

Covered expenses

Deductible

Deductible maximum

Employer contributions

Exclusions and limitations

First-dollar coverage

Group major medical expense insurance

Individual basic hospital-surgical insurance

Integrated deductible

Nondiscrimination

Per cause

Reasonable and customary (R&C)

Reimbursement percentages

Subrogation clause

Supplemental

Tax-favored treatment

Three-month carryover provision

1. What types of treatment or care are sometimes covered by modern medical expense insurance that were not in the past?

2. From 1950 to 1994 what was the percentage increase in private health insurance claim payments?

3. What is the basic difference between major medical and basic hospital-surgical insurance?

4. What are the two kinds of major medical expense plans?

5. What types of groups offer major medical insurance?

6. What is a major cause of the growth of group major medical plans?

7. What percent of employee compensation was medical insurance in 1959? In 1995?

8. What are some of the changes in medical plans designed to slow their rising cost?

9. What categories of people other than employees are usually eligible for coverage?

10. What are the major nondiscrimination requirements in each category?

spouses

pregnancies

age restrictions

people with handicaps

health status

terminating employees

11. Why is the same company usually the carrier for both a basic hospital-surgical plan and a major medical plan?

12. If an insured is covered under a comprehensive major medical plan that has a calendar-year deductible of $500 and then pays 80% of remaining covered expenses, and the insured has a covered expense of $10,000 in a given year, how much does the policy pay?

13. What is a corridor deductible?

14. What does "first-dollar coverage" mean?

15. What kind of plans sometimes have an integrated deductible?

16. How does an integrated deductible work?

17. What is the primary purpose of a deductible?

18. What are three factors that account for the amount of a deductible in a policy?

19. What was the percentage increase in the CPI in the forty years between 1955 and 1995?

20. How do employers persuade employees to accept higher deductibles?

21. Which type of major medical insurnace generally has higher deductibles: group or individual?

22. What type of major medical plans are more apt to have deductibles that must be met over a period of two to three years?

23. What is the difference between all cause and per cause deductibles?

24. Which deductible (all cause or per cause) is used most in group major medical plans?

25. What is a disadvantage of the per cause deductible for the insurer?

26. What two amounts are compared in a variable or sliding deductible?

27. Which of these two amounts is used for the variable or sliding deductible?

28. Which type of major medical plan—group or individual—has variable or sliding deductibles more often? Why?

29. What is the purpose of a three-month carryover provision for deductibles?

30. How does a common accident provision for deductibles work?

31. What type of deductible in group major medical plans is gradually replacing the carryover and common accident provisions?

32. What is the difference between a maximum coinsurance provision and a maximum out-of-pocket provision?

33. Besides helping to reduce premiums, what is the other purpose of deductibles and coinsurance?

34. How do HMOs generally treat deductibles and coinsurance?

35. What is the current trend in setting benefit maximums?

36. What are the two types of benefit maximums?

37. Why does major medical coverage have more coverages than individual hospital-surgical policies?

38. What are three conditions that a group major medical policy expense must meet to be covered?

39. How is the limit on room and board charges set in a group major medical policy?

40. What part of intensive care expenses are covered by group major medical policies?

41. Which of these services would generally be covered by a group major medical policy?

physician   registered nurse

custodial care   X-rays

local ambulance   replacement of artificial limbs

rental of a hospital bed   cost of blood in a blood transfusion

42. Why would a national employer prefer reasonable and customary charges to a fee schedule?

43. What are the four general reasons that some charges are excluded from group major medical plans?

44. To avoid double payments, what three types of charges are either excluded or limited?

45. What rights does a subrogation clause give an insurance company?

46. What are some common items excluded from major medical policies?

47. What two types of injuries are normally excluded?

48. How does the Health Insurance Portability and Accountability Act of 1996 treat pre-existing conditions in group medical plans?

49. How are benefits limited for mental, nervous disorder, alcohol, or drug treatment?

50. What is the exception on limiting benefits for mental health imposed by the Health Insurance Portability and Accountability Act of 1996?

51. What are two other specific treatments that often have limited benefits?

Chapter 2

INDIVIDUAL HOSPITAL-SURGICAL INSURANCE

■ Key Terms

Ancillary charges

Ambulance transportation

Attempted suicide

Coinsurance

Complications of pregnancy

Cosmetic treatment and surgery

Covered expenses

Daily benefits

Daily maximums

Daily room and board

Dental conditions and treatment

Exclusions

Extended care

Health Insurance Portability and
Accountability Act of 1996 (HIPAA)

Home health care

Hospital daily benefit

Ineligible expenses

Intensive care

Intentional self-inflicted injuries

Limitations

Maternity coverage

Maximum benefit period

Mental and nervous conditions

Military duty

Military/government hospitals

Miscellaneous hospital expenses

Occupational illnesses or injuries

Optional benefits rider

Outpatient tests

Physician inhospital expenses

Pre-existing conditions

Primary surgical procedures

Reasonable and customary (R&C)

Secondary surgical procedures

Surgical expenses

Surgical schedule

Therapeutic surgery

Time limit on certain defenses

War and acts of war

Workers' compensation law

1. What types of people are most apt to need and buy individual medical expense insurance?

2. How do group and individual medical expense insurance usually differ in these categories?

covered charges

share of charges borne by insured

limits for single illness or period

3. What types of dependents can usually be covered by individual medical expense policies?

4. What are the two most common ways insurers use to cover hospital room and board?

5. Why are individuals given a choice of how much the policy will pay for hospital room and board?

6. How does the policy reflect the different charges for intensive or critical care expenses?

7. How is the cost of nursing care usually covered?

8. How long does the benefit period typically last?

9. How does a policy determine if a hospital confinement is for the same or a different condition if the insured was discharged from the hospital and then returned to the hospital?

10. Name the types of expenses usually covered by the miscellaneous hospital expense benefit.

11. If a physician's services are required to analyze x-rays or lab results, how are these charges handled?

12. How do different policies express the maximum amount payable for miscellaneous expenses?

13. What benefit generally covers outpatient expenses?

14. What types of outpatient expenses might be covered?

15. Is the miscellaneous expense benefit usually a part of the policy or a rider?

16. What are some ways that outpatient expense benefits are provided?

17. What is coverage of the fees charged by a surgeon called?

18. Where does surgery usually have to be performed to be covered?

19. If a surgeon charges more than the reasonable and customary fee for his/her region, who pays the part of the fee over and above the reasonable and customary level?

20. What are the two ways a policy usually uses to cover a surgeon's expenses?

21. If a fee schedule is used, what are the two ways the schedule shows how much will be paid?

22. If a surgical procedure is performed that is not on the fee schedule, how are benefits determined?

23. If two different surgical procedures are performed during the same operation, what benefits are paid?

24. Why is pregnancy treated differently than illnesses and injuries?

25. If pregnancy is covered, how is coverage generally expressed in the policy?

26. If pregnancy is covered by a separate rider, how is coverage generally expressed?

27. How are complications of pregnancy handled?

28. Is a cesarean section usually considered a complication or part of a regular pregnancy?

29. What is the coverage called that provides benefits to cover the expenses of an attending physician in the hospital?

30. What provision covers the expenses of postsurgical followup visits by a physician?

31. What are two ways that policies limit physician inhospital expenses?

32. Why do insurers like to provide continued or home health care benefits?

33. Under what conditions are nursing home charges covered?

34. What is generally required for a facility to be eligible for extended care facility coverage?

35. How is reimbursement for an extended care facility limited?

36. What is usually necessary for home health care to be covered?

37. How is home health care reimbursed?

38. How is full time nursing care at home covered by the home health care benefit?

39. What limitations are put on charges for ambulance services?

40. If a hospital charges for an ambulance that brings a person to the hospital for inpatient care, which benefit pays the expense?

41. What are some common exclusions and limitations in an individual hospital expense policy?

42. What is a common definition of pre-existing conditions?

43. What new restrictions does HIPAA put on insurers regarding pre-existing conditions in individual medical expense policies?

44. What are the four conditions a person has to meet to be subject to the HIPAA restrictions on pre-existing conditions?

45. How does an insurer protect itself from covering medical expenses for a condition whose treatment is subject to a certain amount of elective timing?

46. What are some examples of these specified common conditions?

47. How does HIPAA affect the specified common condition exclusion?

48. Why is it difficult for insurers to enforce the self-inflicted injury exclusion?

49. Are intentional actions that result in accidental injury covered? Why or why not?

50. If a person covered by an individual medical expense policy enlists in the armed forces, what happens to the policy? What happens to the policy when the person is discharged from the armed forces? What happens to the premiums due?

51. If a person is in the military part-time (ROTC, National Guard, Reserves), what happens to individual coverage?

52. What did the Veterans Administration Amendment of 1986 require insurers to do?

53. Why are injuries covered by workers' compensation laws usually excluded from coverage in individual policies?

54. How do individual medical expense policies treat conditions like heart disease and high blood pressure that may be work-related, but are difficult to claim from workers' compensation?

55. What types of dental work would be covered by an individual medical expense policy?

56. What are five common ways an insurer limits its risk for coverage of mental or nervous disorders?

57. The same operation could be considered cosmetic surgery or therapeutic surgery. What is the criterion for deciding which it is?

58. When would surgery to correct birth defects be covered?

Chapter 3

MARKETING AND SELLING MEDICAL EXPENSE INSURANCE

■ Key Terms

Agent

Association sales

Broker

Copayment

Customers

Deductible

Direct selling

Distribution

Employee benefit plan

Errors and omissions (E&O) insurance

Fee-for-service

Field office system

Health insurance purchasing cooperative (HIPC)

Health maintenance organization (HMO)

Indemnity

Managed care

Market

Market research

Marketing mix

Nondomestic market

Out-of-pocket maximum

Payroll deduction programs

Point of sale (POS)

Preferred provider organization (PPO)

Price

Product

Promotion

Risk pools

1. What is market research?

2. What does a marketing plan attempt to do?

3. In general, what is the difference between agents and brokers?

4. Because an individual has less knowledge about plan designs, an insurance company's reputation, or an individual agent or broker, what tends to dominate his or her purchase decision?

5. What can a good agent or broker do to help an individual choose a policy?

6. What is the tradeoff a consumer has to make to pay fewer out-of-pocket expenses for health insurance?

7. What are four ways the financing and delivery of health care is integrated under managed care?

8. What are the two extreme ends of medical expense products?

9. Who shares the risk in a managed care capitation setting?

10. How are indemnity health insurance and managed care marketed differently?

11. What type of health care is emphasized in managed care, but not indemnity insurance?

12. What are the potential problems in pricing a product too low?

13. What is the effect of group medical expense plans where the employer pays most of the premiums?

14. How does better medical technology increase the cost of health care?

15. How does regulation increase the cost of health care?

16. What is the purpose of state risk pools?

17. What is a "direct writer"?

18. What are three ways agents are compensated?

19. How are brokers compensated?

20. Are agents and brokers employees of an insurance company?

21. What is an HIPC?

22. Why is medical expense insurance rarely sold directly through the mail or by phone?

23. What types of health insurance are more apt to be sold directly by mail or phone?

24. In which areas does the World Wide Web show promise as a marketing tool?

25. How are products sold through payroll deduction programs different than other insurance where the employer deducts part of the premium from the employees' pay?

26. What has caused the market for payroll deduction policies for medical insurance to decline?

27. What other organizations offer individual health insurance?

28. Why is customer service becoming more important to the insurance industry?

29. What is it called when employee compensation programs are tied to customer survey results?

30. What two major issues are involved in the private insurance vs. government insurance debate?

31. What are some other nondomestic market opportunities?

Chapter 4

PRICING MEDICAL EXPENSE INSURANCE

■ Key Terms

Age at entry rates

Age-banded rates

Aggregate stop-loss insurance

Area rating factors

Claim costs

Claim reserve

Coinsurance

Contingency margin

Cost containment features

Deductible

Development method

Experience rating

Fixed retention

Frequency

Fully insured plan

Guaranteed issue

Guaranteed renewable

Health Insurance Portability and Accountability Act of 1996 (HIPAA)

Incurred but not reported reserves

Lapse rate

Loss ratio method

Minimum premium plan

Morbidity

Mortality

Noncancellable

Nonrenewable for stated reasons only

Optionally renewable

Partial experience rating

Pending reserves

Persistency

Pooling

Pre-existing condition

Premium rate

Rate manual

Rate stabilization reserve

Rating classes

Retention

Retrospective premium arrangement

Self-insured plan

Severity

Small group laws

Specific stop-loss insurance

State-mandated benefits

Stop-loss insurance

Trend

Variable retention

1. Why are there no standard tables to determine medical claim costs?

2. What are the basic components of the premium rate?

3. What two variables affect claim costs in medical expense insurance?

4. How do you calculate the overall claim cost for a policy?

5. What demographic factors are considered when calculating claim costs for each benefit?

6. What is the purpose of the contingency margin?

7. What is the purpose of a claim reserve?

8. Why is the estimate of incurred but not paid claims particularly important for group insurance?

9. How is the loss ratio calculated?

10. What are the six major types of expenses common to medical expense insurance?

11. How is overhead generally allocated?

12. What accounts for the small profit margins in medical expense insurance in the last few years?

13. What three measures are used to account for terminations?

14. How is the lapse rate calculated?

15. How is persistency measured?

16. How important is mortality in calculating the lapse rate?

17. What age groups tend to have more lapses?

18. How do lapse rates vary with the length of time the policy has been in force?

19. How do premium increases affect claims experience?

20. How are claim costs estimated in group vs. individual medical expense insurance?

21. How do price trends affect rate tables?

22. What is the best source of data for individual morbidity tables?

23. Where are other statistics found?

24. What demographic factors affect manual rates?

25. What source do actuaries usually use to classify industries?

26. What is a loading factor?

27. How can plan design affect premiums?

28. What are medical audits of hospital bills looking for?

29. What is a common lifetime maximum for a hospital expense policy?

30. What are the four standard renewability options in individual health insurance?

31. What kind of renewability does HIPAA require?

32. What are the components of price trends?

33. What is cost shifting?

34. How do new medical technologies affect medical costs?

35. How does the minimum participation requirement vary between large and small groups?

36. Why are insurers less concerned with participation in a large group plan?

37. Why is there a tradeoff between higher underwriting costs and higher claim costs?

38. Why is it possible to consider good underwriting as only a temporary solution to higher claim costs?

39. What are pending reserves designed to cover?

40. What is the other claim reserve other than pending reserves?

41. How do you calculate claim reserves using the loss ratio method?

42. What are the advantages and disadvantages of the development or lag method compared to the loss ratio method of calculating claim reserves?

43. What is involved in using the development or lag method?

44. What is meant by claim runoff?

45. How are rating classes used?

46. What are the six common characteristics of an individual rating structure?

47. For which of these characteristics does the law require the insurer to use the same rate for all insureds, even though actuarial evidence shows a difference in claims between one group and another?

48. Why do insurers use a substandard rate class?

49. What are the three commonly used age-rating methods?

50. Which of the age-rating methods has the worst persistency?

51. When is it best to use level rates?

52. What two characteristics make claim costs fairly predictable in group medical insurance?

53. Why do insurers use experience rating for groups?

54. How can smaller groups take advantage of experience rating?

55. What is blending?

56. How is a blended rate calculated?

57. If the experience rate for a group is $400 and the manual rate is $500, and the group's experience is 50 percent credible, what is the blended rate?

58. What does retention include?

59. How is a rate stabilization reserve funded?

60. What is the rate stabilization reserve used for?

61. If a policyholder cancels the policy before the rate stabilization reserve is used, who usually gets the money?

62. What is the incurred claim loss ratio compared to when analyzing policy experience?

63. When should loss ratios be higher: in the first few years of a policy's life or several years later?

64. How does a minimum premium contract help a policyholder?

65. Under a minimum premium contract, where does the expected claims portion of the premium go?

66. In a retrospective premium arrangement, what happens if the plan cost is greater than the premiums paid?

67. Why are administration fees in an ASO contract often less than retention fees in standard insurance?

68. How can a self-insured employer protect itself against large claim losses?

69. What is the difference between aggregate stop-loss insurance and specific stop-loss insurance?

70. What are some typical mandated benefits?

71. What sorts of issues are addressed by the NAIC model acts on small groups?

72. What standards are applied to increases in individual medical expense insurance premiums?

73. How does HIPAA affect renewability of small group policies?

Chapter 5

MEDICAL EXPENSE CONTRACT PROVISIONS

■ Key Terms

Benefits payable

Certificate of insurance

COBRA (Consolidated Omnibus Budget Reconciliation Act) continuance

Consideration

Continuance of coverage

Continuance of insurance

Contract

Conversion

Coordination of benefits

Cover page

Covered expenses

Effective date

Eligible dependent

Eligible employee

Eligibility date

Expenses not covered

Extension of benefits

Facility of payment

Financial rider

General rider

Grace period

HMO transfer

Insuring clause

Limitations

Managed indemnity programs

Misstatement

Policyholder

Precertification review

Premium provision

Renewal provision

Retroactive rate reduction

Right to examine

Schedule of insurance

Termination of coverage

Utilization review

1. What is the advantage of combining all the coverages into one group policy?

2. Where would you find the issue date and effective date of the policy?

3. What is a participating policy?

4. What is it called when a certificate is issued without reference to any specific insured individual?

5. If a new employee wants to join a group health plan, what are conditions for coverage?

6. When is the effective date of insurance for an employee entering a contributory plan?

7. Why does a policy want a new employee actively at work on the effective date of the policy?

8. Under what conditions can an employee enroll late without incurring late enrollment penalties?

9. What does HIPAA say about late enrollees?

10. What are the usual categories of dependents?

11. Where are summaries of plan features found in the contract?

12. When does coverage end for employees?

13. When can premiums be changed in group plans?

14. What are the exceptions to this?

15. Under HIPAA, what circumstances are necessary before the insurer can terminate a group policy?

16. What is generally done in the case of a clerical error or misstatement?

17. What happens to premiums and claims during the grace period?

18. Who keeps a signed copy of the group policy?

19. How are amendments to a policy made?

20. What does a combination rider do?

21. What is the relationship between the certificate of insurance and the insurance policy?

22. Where is the type of loss the policy covers stated?

23. What are the managed care provisions that are sometimes written into indemnity health insurance today?

24. What is the purpose of a coordination of benefits provision?

25. What happens if the insured is totally disabled on the date coverage ends?

26. Who is the policyholder in group insurance? In individual insurance?

27. In an individual policy, how long does the insured have to return the policy for a complete refund of premiums?

28. In an individual policy, what happens to the dependents' coverage if the insured dies?

29. If an individual medical expense policy is reinstated, when would it start covering sickness?

Chapter 6

UNDERWRITING MEDICAL EXPENSE INSURANCE

■ Key Terms

Acceptable group

Adverse selection

Census data

Contributory plan

Coordination of benefits (COB)

Credibility

Discriminatory

Duplicate coverage

Eligibility

Eligible group

Employment conditions

Enrollment

Evidence of insurability

Excess risk

Insurability

Key employees

Late entrants

Medical underwriting

Minimum participation

Multiple employer trust (MET)

Noncontributory plan

Overutilization

Participation

Persistency

Quota share

Reinsurer

Renewal underwriting

Resolicitation

Risk

Single employer group

Spread of risk

Stop-loss

Taft-Hartley health and welfare trust plans

Transferred risk

Turnover

Underwriter

1. What is the single greatest threat to the underwriting process?

2. What is adverse selection?

3. What is the difference between morbidity and mortality?

4. Why have medical advances decreased mortality but increased morbidity?

5. What are the two organizational structures used in setting up an underwriting department?

6. What is a potential drawback of having too many separate underwriting units?

7. What is a potential drawback of having a product-line organization of the underwriting department?

8. What is an advantage of regionalization of underwriting?

9. Why does the field agent rely on the underwriter?

10. If HIPAA forbids an insurer from rejecting a small group application, why is underwriting still necessary?

11. Why is there more morbidity in small groups?

12. What expenses might be higher as a percentage of premium for small groups (besides claims)?

13. What are some occupations that might have higher morbidity than average?

14. Why are part-time, seasonal, and temporary employees usually excluded from coverage?

15. What might be a disadvantage of a group with younger-than-average employees?

16. What is the relationship between earnings and use of medical services?

17. In examining geographic location as a factor, what might cancel out higher charges in a region?

18. In a group plan, what is eligibility related to?

19. What is a typical probationary period before a new employee is eligible for group health insurance?

20. If an employer requests a plan with minimum benefits, what problems might this be a sign of?

21. What is the difference between contributory and noncontributory plans?

22. Why are noncontributory groups favored by an underwriter?

23. Why is an insurer reluctant to issue a policy to an employer who allows employees to pay 100 percent of the premiums?

24. How can claim experience for a small group be normalized by an underwriter?

25. Why does an underwriter want to see the previous health insurance policy of an employer who is applying for group coverage?

26. What are discontinuance and replacement (D&R) laws?

27. Why do underwriters like level commissions more than high first-year commissions?

28. What are some typical acquisition costs?

29. When are the acquisition costs included in the premium?

30. What is the risk an employer takes who self insures with a stop-loss provision (other than incurring claim costs)?

31. What should an insurer be wary of who is approached by an employer who wants to change from self-insured to insured?

32. In terms of plan design, compare the options of a large group plan to an individual policy.

33. What does the underwriter evaluate for any current or prior condition?

34. If accidents on the job are covered by workers' compensation, why is an underwriter concerned with an applicant's occupation?

35. What can an underwriter do to avoid the extra risk of a dangerous avocation?

36. Why is identifying moral hazards important to an underwriter?

37. What indicates the possibility of moral hazard?

38. Why would an underwriter be suspicious if the applicant tried to exclude some dependents from coverage?

39. Approximately what percentage of applications are rated standard, declined, or modified?

40. How can policies be modified to insure applicants that might be declined otherwise?

41. Which of these approaches is generally most acceptable to the applicant?

42. What are some underwriting problems particular to Taft-Hartley groups?

43. How do unions decide who is eligible for health insurance under a Taft-Hartley plan?

44. What has reduced the importance of METs?

45. Why are underwriters concerned with association groups and franchise groups?

46. Why do medical expense insurers tend to avoid public employers?

47. Why are social and fraternal organizations usually classified as ineligible risks?

48. What are the four main concerns of the underwriter when reviewing the plan of benefits?

49. What is the percentage range that cost containment features save?

50. How much extra administrative costs do cost containment features add?

51. What incentives does a primary care physician have to reduce referrals to specialists and hospital admissions?

52. Who assumes the risk under a global capitation agreement?

53. Under what conditions will an insurer reinstate part or all of the maximum lifetime limit?

54. If participation in a group plan falls below the minimum level, what can the insurer do?

55. What percentage of additional employees need to sign up during a resolicitation period?

56. Why would an insurer not want a renewal notice period longer than 30 days?

57. Why do HMOs tend to have longer periods of guaranteed rates than indemnity insurers?

58. What are the circumstances that allow an insurer to non-renew an individual health policy?

59. If an employer wants to add an additional class of employees to the policy, what does an underwriter want to know?

60. What does a ceding company do?

61. What is the difference between the two main types of reinsurance?

Chapter 7

MEDICAL EXPENSE POLICY ADMINISTRATION

■ Key Terms

Accounting statement

Administration manual

Administrative services only (ASO)

Audit

Automated voice response system (AVRS)

Case

Code of Ethical Practices

Continuing administration

Customer service

Customer service representative

Digital imaging (document scanning)

Electronic record

Eligibility

Employee information

Employee Retirement Income Security Act (ERISA)

Group information

Insurer-administered

Microfilm/microfiche

Multiple employer trust (MET)

Negotiated trusteeship

New insurance account

Overdue premium collection

Paper file

Plan administrator

Policyholder

Professional association

Recordkeeping

Reserve fund

Self-administered plan

Service record

Taft-Hartley health and welfare trust plan

Third-party administrator (TPA)

Trade association

Welcome letter

1. What are the two levels of records for a group policy?

2. In self-administered plans, who keeps the eligibility files?

3. What is the purpose of the insurer's administration manual?

4. What is the purpose of the welcome letter?

5. What are the disadvantages of paper files?

6. What is the most popular alternative to paper files?

7. What are statistics on policyholders used for?

8. In individual health insurance, who has the main responsibility for making sure the insured knows how to file claims, etc.?

9. Why is customer service so important in insurance?

10. What is necessary for the success of a company's customer service?

11. What are the five concerns of insurance customers?

12. What are some ways insurers measure customer service performance?

13. What is a new system insurers use to answer customer calls for information?

14. Who prepares the premium statement in a self-administered plan?

15. Is premium due for coverage during the grace period?

16. If the policyholder does not pay premium due, can individuals covered by the policy still convert to individual policies?

17. Under HIPAA, what does an insurer have to issue to each certificate-holder in a group plan that terminates?

18. Why is customer service essential to retaining agents and brokers?

19. Who are internal customers?

20. Who can administer multi-group plans?

21. What are two main differences between administration of association groups and small groups?

22. What are some special administrative problems that might arise with trade association cases?

23. What additional reserves are needed for trade association plans?

24. What is the purpose of certifying the employment status of the insured to an association?

25. What are the differences in administration between professional associations and trade associations?

26. What are some state regulatory problems with professional association policies?

27. Who can administer a negotiated trusteeship plan?

28. What is special about the effective date of a policy in negotiated trusteeship plans?

29. What is the purpose of the reserve fund in a negotiated trusteeship plan?

30. How often does an insurer have to furnish an accounting statement to the policyholder in a welfare trust plan?

31. How many employees does a typical employer in a MET have?

32. In an MET plan, what is the role of the trustee?

33. How do insurers generally pay TPAs?

34. What are the ways an employer pays an insurer under an ASO contract?

35. Why would budgeting be more difficult under an ASO arrangement (aside from the variations in the claims themselves)?

36. What makes a self-insured plan subject to trust requirement under ERISA?

37. What types of information are in a summary plan description required by ERISA?

38. Who does a plan subject to ERISA have to file an annual report (form 5500) with?

Chapter 8

MEDICAL EXPENSE CLAIM ADMINISTRATION

■ Key Terms

Assignment

Authorization to release information

Auto-adjudicate

Breach of contract

Card-only approach

Claim-kit approach

Claim services only (CSO)

Coinsurance

Compensatory damages

Coordination of benefits (COB)

Current Procedural Terminology (CPT)

Deductible

Direct submission

Duplicate coverage inquiry (DCI)

Electronic data interchange (EDI)

Electronic funds transfer (EFT)

Explanation of benefits (EOB)

Field office claim administration

Home office claim administration

International Claims Association (ICA)

International Classification of Diseases (CD)

Lifetime maximum

Maximum benefit

Order of benefits determination (OBD)

Policyholder submission

Prevailing Healthcare Charges System (PHCS)

Pre-existing condition

Punitive damages

Reasonable and customary (R&C) charges

Third-party administrator

1. How are claims submitted under the direct submission or certification method?

2. What does assignment of benefits mean?

3. What is the difference between the claim-kit and the card-only approaches?

4. Why is the card-only approach more expensive to administer?

5. What is the advantage of home office claim administration?

6. What is the advantage of field office claim administration?

7. If a TPA administers claims, whose money does it use to pay the claims?

8. Who generally selects and pays the TPA?

9. What are the advantages of using a TPA?

10. What are the disadvantages of using a TPA?

11. What services might be provided in an ASO agreement but not a CSO agreement?

12. How much is a family deductible?

13. What are the features of a maximum benefit provision in a major medical policy?

14. Who publishes the Physicians' Current Procedural Terminology (CPT)?

15. What is *ICD-9-CM?* Who publishes it?

16. Which code is used on hospital bills?

17. What is the typical definition of customary charges?

18. How is this different than a reasonable charge?

19. What do E codes describe?

20. How are reasonable and customary charges used in conjunction with scheduled coverages?

21. What are the two methods of generating a representative array of charges by procedure and area?

22. Which method does PHCS use?

23. What are relative values intended to reflect?

24. How are conversion factors calculated?

25. What law governs claim appeals in group plans?

26. Under the NAIC model regulation, what governs which plan is primary in the coordination of benefits if only one plan has a COB provision?

27. Which plan is primary if both plans have a COB provision?

28. What is the birthday rule for determining which plan is primary in covering dependents of parents who are married and living together?

29. Which plan is primary in covering dependents if one plan uses the birthday rule and the other uses the gender rule?

30. What is the priority of plans where the parents of dependents are divorced?

31. What is the active/inactive employee rule?

32. What is the continuation coverage rule?

33. If none of the above rules apply, which plan is primary?

34. Who is the primary source for information about other health insurance?

35. What is the time limit most insurers impose on themselves to resolve COB issues?

36. How does the NAIC COB model regulation treat expenses that may be covered under one policy, but not another?

37. How can the benefit savings with the secondary insurer be used to the advantage of the insured?

38. What is the maintenance of benefits approach to COB?

39. When does an insurer typically check an insured for pre-existing conditions?

40. Under HIPAA, what does an insurer have to do before denying payment of claims for pre-existing conditions in a group policy?

41. How does HIPAA change the way insurers administer the pre-existing condition provision?

42. What are the ICA principles relating to paying claims?

43. What do most misrepresentations involve?

44. Where is the burden of proof in a contested claim case?

45. Who should get the benefit of the doubt in settling questionable claims?

46. What are the three levels in an insurance claim lawsuit?

47. What is necessary for a court to award compensatory damages?

48. What is the purpose of punitive damages?

49. When were extra-contractual damages first awarded?

50. What needs to be proved to get punitive damages?

51. What precedent did *Pilot Life Insurance Company vs. Dedeaux* set?

52. What should a good claim examiner refrain from doing when processing a claim?

53. If a claim is denied, what else has to accompany the denial?

54. What is the goal of EDI in the health insurance industry?

55. Approximately how many medical claims are submitted in the U.S. annually?

56. How much would a complete conversion to EDI save the health care industry per year?

57. How much growth was there in receiving electronic claims between 1990 and 1995 according to HIAA surveys?

58. What are some of the advantages of switching to EDI?

Chapter 9

MEDICAL EXPENSE INDUSTRY ISSUES

■ Key Terms

Cost trends

Employee Retirement Income Security Act (ERISA)

Health Insurance Portability and Accountability Act of 1996 (HIPAA)

Health insurance purchasing cooperatives (HIPCs)

Managed care

Medical savings accounts

Medicare Part A

Medicare Part B

Medicare reform

Medigap

Multiple employer welfare arrangements (MEWAs)

National Association of Insurance Commissioners (NAIC)

Out-of-pocket spending

Provider-sponsored network plans (PSNs)

Self-insurance

Underwriting cycle

1. What are the major changes that have taken place in health insurance over the last 20 years?

2. How are some Blue Cross plans changing?

3. What are some drawbacks to state regulation?

4. What trend did ERISA encourage?

5. What was the percentage of employees covered by employer-sponsored health plans that were self-insured in 1995?

6. What type of abuse is possible in self-insured plans but not standard indemnity health insurance?

7. What alternate distribution system for insurance is emerging?

8. How have some banks interpreted the November 1996 statement by the Comptroller of the Currency?

9. What other insurance opportunity has been created for banks by HIPAA?

10. What do many small employers want?

11. What has happened to the cost of health services in the last several years?

12. Why do consumers report a different picture?

13. How could the underwriting cycle be responsible for lower premium increases in the last few years?

14. What are some other explanations of lower premium increases?

15. Summarize the arguments for and against managed care being able to continue to keep health care spending under control.

16. What are some challenges that lie ahead?

17. What are the elements in Medicare reform proposals that concern insurers the most?

18. What is the insurers' objection to provider-sponsored networks?

19. What do insurers think will happen if Medicare supplement policies become guaranteed issue?

SAMPLE EXAMINATION

HIAA examinations may have three types of questions:

1) Positive Multiple Choice

Each question or statement below is followed by four answers lettered A, B, C, and D. Select the one answer which is best in each case. Completely fill in the bubble for the corresponding letters (A, B, C, or D) in the proper space on the answer sheet.

Sample Question:

The name of the ocean located between Europe and Africa on the east and North and South America on the west is the

    A. Arctic.
    B. Atlantic.*
    C. Indian.
    D. Pacific.

*Correct Answer.

2) Multiple Option

Each of the following questions contains an introduction followed by several expressions identified as I, II, and III. For each question, determine which one of the combinations identified as A, B, C, or D is most correct and completely fill in the bubble for the corresponding letter in the proper space on the answer sheet.

Sample Question:

Which of the states below border Canada?

    I. Alaska.
   II. Iowa.
   III. New York.

    A. III only
    B. I and II only
    C. I and III only*
    D. I, II, and III

*Correct Answer

Singular or plural grammatical form in the question does not imply a singular or plural answer. In the example, "Which of the states below border Canada?" the structure is plural, but the answer may be either singular (one state) or plural (two or more states).

3) Negative Multiple Choice

Each question is followed by four answers (A, B, C, and D). Select the answer which best completes the sentence and completely fill in the bubble for the corresponding letter (A, B, C, or D) in the proper space on the answer sheet.

Sample Question:

All the cities listed below are national capitals EXCEPT

    A. London.
    B. Paris.
    C. Sydney.*
    D. Washington.

*Correct Answer

The sample examination below (10 questions) is not meant to test your knowledge of the subject, but to show you the types of questions that might be asked. Do not use your score on this sample test to predict your score on the actual exam, since the number of questions is too few to be meaningful. The actual examination will contain 100 or fewer multiple choice questions, equally weighted, and have a time limit of two and half hours or less. HIAA examinations have been highly reliable in the past, almost always yielding reliability coefficients of .90 or better.

1. If an insured has a comprehensive major medical plan with an annual deductible of $500 and a copayment provision requiring the insured to pay 20% of allowable expenses, how much does the policy pay if the insured has $5,000 worth of allowable expenses in a given year?

    A. $900.
    B. $3,600.
    C. $4,100.
    D. $5,000.

2. In a hospital-surgical policy, how is the cost of inpatient nursing care covered?

    A. Supplement to surgical expense.
    B. Part of miscellaneous expenses.
    C. Grouped with physician fees.
    D. Included in room and board.

3. If a person is cleaning a gun and it goes off and injures the person's foot, would medical care be covered or excluded under a typical hospital-surgical policy? Why or why not?

    A. Covered—injury was not intentional.
    B. Covered—all injuries, however caused, are covered.
    C. Excluded—self-inflicted injury.
    D. Excluded—act of war.

4. Who shares the financial risk with the insurer in a managed care capitation setting?

    A. Policyholder.
    B. Provider.
    C. Patient.
    D. Employer.

5. Which of these age groups tend to have more lapsed health policies than average?

   I. The young.
   II. Those near retirement.
   III. The middle aged.

   A. I and II only
   B. I and III only
   C. II and III only
   D. I, II, and III

6. What part of the policy explains what type of loss the policy covers?

   A. Cover page.
   B. Riders.
   C. Claim forms.
   D. Insuring clause.

7. What determines eligibility in a group health plan?
   A. Age.
   B. Income.
   C. Employment.
   D. Gender.

8. Under HIPAA, what does an insurer have to issue to each certificate-holder in a group plan that is terminated?

   A. A refund of unearned premium.
   B. A certificate of the length of past coverage.
   C. Notice of continued coverage under COBRA.
   D. A receipt for claims paid.

9. What are some advantages of using a TPA?

   I. Usually has lower administrative fees than an insurer.
   II. Has more consistent interpretations of policy language.
   III. Can give local service when the insurer's office is far away.

   A. I and III only
   B. I and II only
   C. I, II, and III
   D. II and III only

10. What trend was encouraged by ERISA?

   A. Growth of managed care.
   B. Cost-shifting to private payers.
   C. Growth of self-insured plans.
   D. Outsourcing of administration to TPAs.

Answers to sample test:

1. B
2. D
3. A
4. B
5. A
6. D
7. C
8. B
9. A
10. C